Letterland ELT

Hello! I'm Monkey.
What's your name?

My name is

T0347181

Hello! I'm Clever Cat.

 c...

I start words like...

cat   **car**   **cake**

Sing and point

Find...

Find...

3

Listen and say

Hello! I'm Monkey.

Listen, chant and point

1 one

2 two

3 three

Hello! I'm Annie Apple.

Track 9

 a...

I start words like...

apple   **acrobat**   **ant**

Sing and point ♪

Track 10

6

Find...

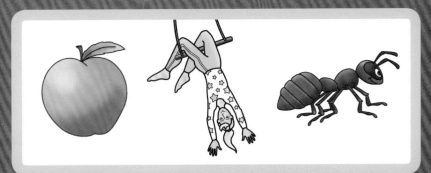

Appletree Avenue

Meet Mr A!

Listen, chant and point

eyes

nose

mouth

Listen, chant and point

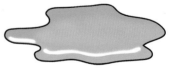

red   yellow   green

Colour, cut and play

Give each child a set of numbers like the above to colour in and cut out.

Memory game

9

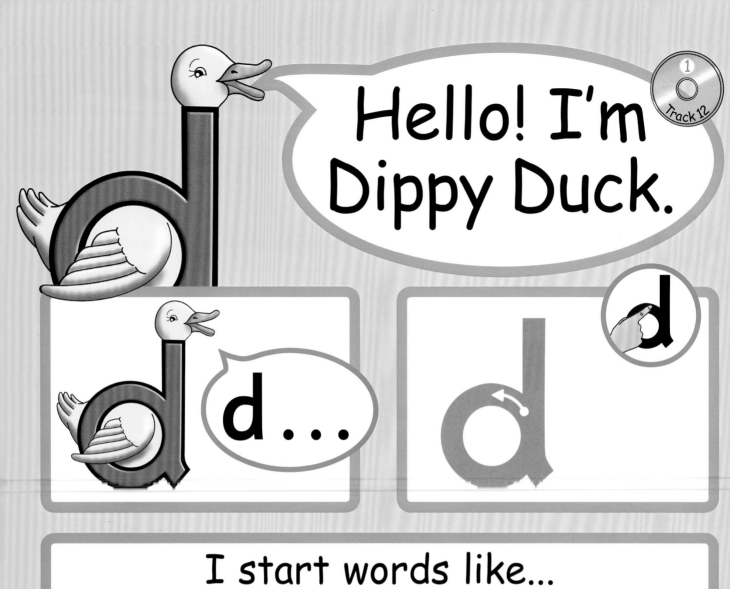

Hello! I'm Dippy Duck.

d...

I start words like...

duck   dinosaur   dog

Sing and point ♪

10

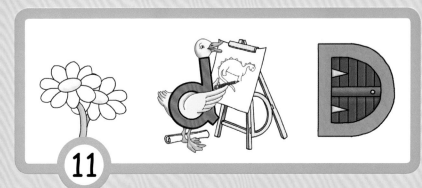

11

Listen, point and say

1
Track 14

 d...  a...  d...

d   a   d

da d

dad

My dad

Chant!

12

Finger trace

Now count with me!

13

Hello! I'm Harry Hat Man.

h...

I start words like...

hat   horse   house

Sing and point ♫

14

Find...

Find...

15

Finger trace

Count!

Track 18

16

Sing and do

"**This** is my hand!"

"**These** are my hands!"

"**This** is my foot!"

"**These** are my feet!"

17

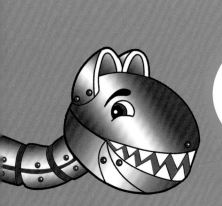

Hello! I'm Munching Mike.

m...

m

I start words like...

magnet **monkey** **milk**

Sing and point

18

Find...

Find...

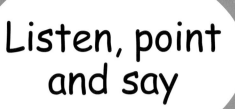

Listen, point and say

"I'm hungry!"

"Eat!"

"I'm thirsty!"

"Drink!"

20

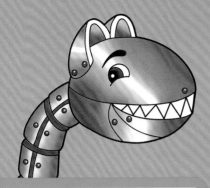

Track 23

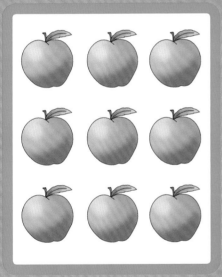

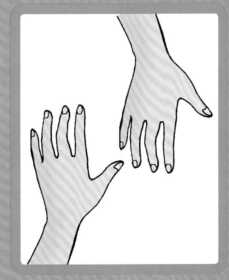

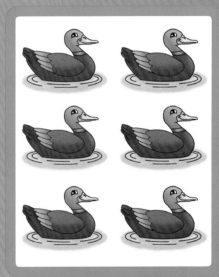

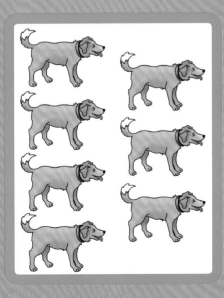

21

Hello! I'm Talking Tess.

t...

t

I start words like...

 tiger

 telephone

 ten

 Sing and point

22

Find...

Find...

Listen, point and say

 c...

 a...

 t...

c · a · t ·

ca⟶ t ·

cat⟶

24

Finger trace

Count!

Track 27

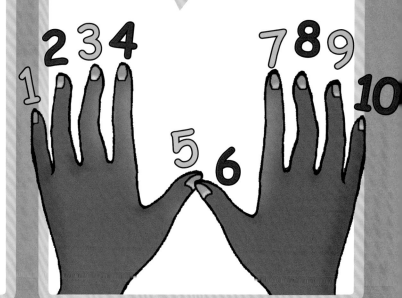

Sing and play

Track 28

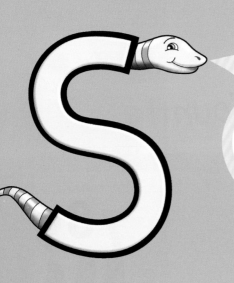

Hello! I'm Sammy Snake.

Track 29

s...

I start words like...

snake

sun

7

seven

Sing and point

Track 30

26

Find...

Find...

27

Listen

1

2

Listen, point and say

 s...  a...  d...

s a d

1

2

3

4

5

Happy face, sad face!

How are you?

I'm sad!

How are you?

I'm happy!

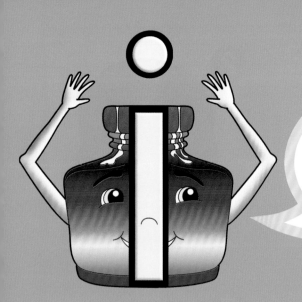

Hello! I'm Impy Ink.

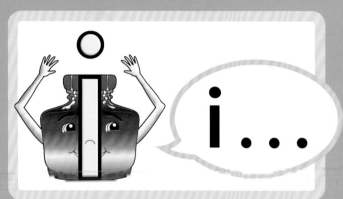

i...

I start words like...

insect

ink

in

Sing and point

Find...

Meet Mr I!

Sing and point

in

on

in

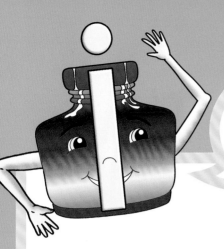

Listen, count and say

"How many legs?"

33

Hello! I'm Noisy Nick.

Track 37

n...

I start words like...

nest   **nine**   **nut**

Sing and point

Track 38

Find...

Count!

35

"How old are you?"

"I am 9 years old!"

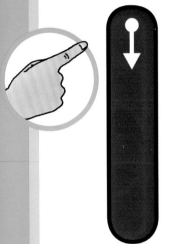

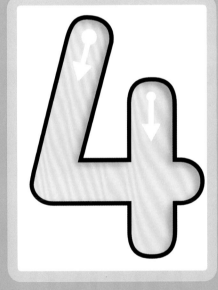

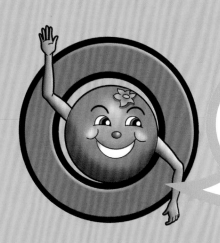

Hello! I'm Oscar Orange.

O...

I start words like...

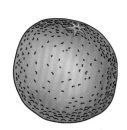  

orange **octopus** **ostrich**

Sing and point

38

Find...

Meet Mr O!

39

Listen, chant and point

triangle

circle

square

Listen and say

Listen and say

Listen, point and say

o...   o...   o...   o...

a...   a...   a...   a...

o...   a...   o...   a...

o...

41

Hello! I'm Peter Puppy.

I start words like...

 **paint**

 **parrot**

 **pig**

Sing and point

Find...

Listen, chant and point

person

people

Listen and point

Hello! I'm Yo-yo Man.

y...

I start words like...

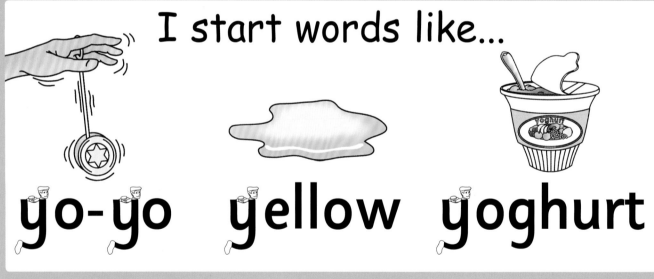

yo-yo   yellow   yoghurt

Sing and point

46

Hello! I'm Golden Girl.

g...

I start words like...

green   **grapes**   **goat**

Sing and point

47

Listen point and say

big

little

little

big

Listen, point and say

Listen, finger trace and say

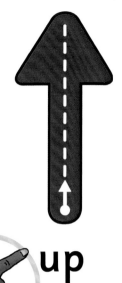

up

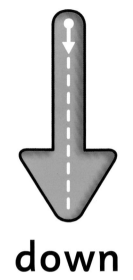

down

around

down

up

around

around

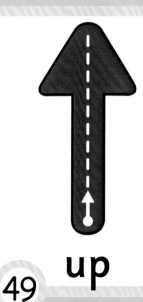

up

down

Hello! I'm Eddy Elephant.

e...

I start words like...

 elephant  egg  elbow

Sing and point 🎵

Hello! I'm Uppy Umbrella.

u...

I start words like...

umbrella

up

under

Sing and point ♫

51

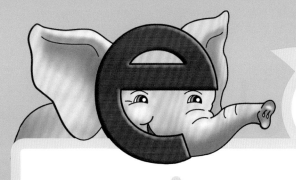

The vowels!

Listen, point and say

t...

e...

n...

t.

e.

n.

ten

10

u...

p...

up

Hello! I'm Kicking King.

k...

k

I start words like...

key   kangaroo   kite

Sing and point 🎵

Track 14

Hello! I'm Quarrelsome Queen.

I start words like...

quill   question   quilt

Sing and point

Point and say

Quarrelsome Queen's Questions!

Listen, point and say

 d...  u...  ck...

du   ck

→

·

duck →

ducks →

·

ducks →

57

Hello! I'm Firefighter Fred.

f...

f

I start words like...

fire   flowers   fish

Sing and point

f

58

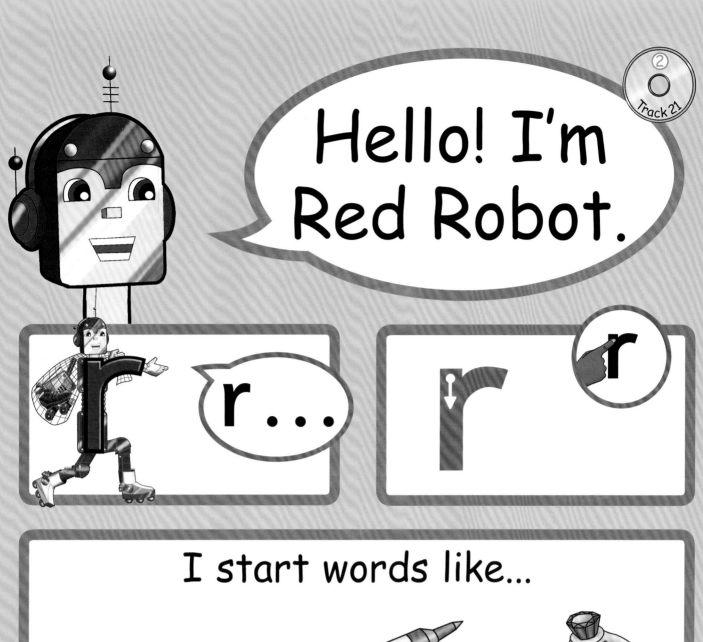

Hello! I'm Red Robot.

r...

I start words like...

red   rocket   ring

Sing and point ♩♫

r

59

Listen, point and say

1

2

3

4

5

6

7

8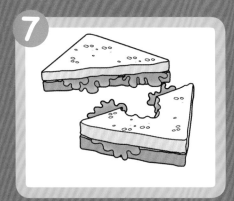

9

60

Listen, point and say

 s...

 u...

 n...

sun

➡

 r...

 u...

 n...

run

➡

Hello! I'm Lucy Lamp Light.

l...

I start words like...

lamp   lighthouse   leg

Sing and point

62

Hello! I'm Vicky Violet.

 V...

I start words like...

 vase  vegetables  van

 Sing and point

63

Hello! I'm Jumping Jim.

j...

j

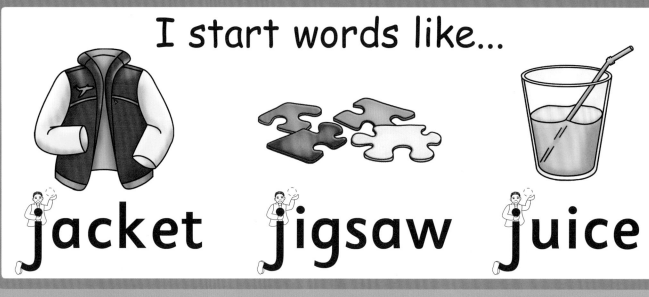

I start words like...

jacket jigsaw juice

Sing and point ♫ j

Hello! I'm Bouncy Ben.

b...

I start words like...

 ball 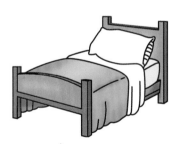 bed  blue

Sing and point ♫

67

Listen, point and say

Track 35

b   e   d

be d
→

bed
→

r   e   d

re d
→

red
→

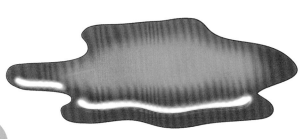

69

Hello! I'm Walter Walrus.

W...

I start words like...

 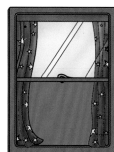 

water window web

Sing and point ♪

Hello! I'm Fix-it Max.

k-ss...

X x

I am at the end of words like...

box fox six

Sing and point

71

Hello! I'm Zig Zag Zebra.

z . . .

I start words like...

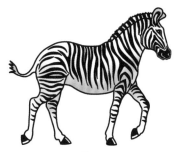
zebra

zero

zoo

Sing and point ♪

72

Say all the letter sounds

a b
c d e f g
h i j k l
m n o p q
r s t u v
w x y z

Listen!

sh

Listen, say and point

shell

ship

splash

fish

Say and point

ch

Listen, say and point

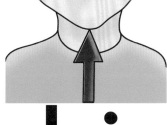

chin

chick

children

bench

Revision

Numbers

 one

 two

 three

 four

 five

 six

 seven

 eight

 nine

ten

Colours

 red

 yellow

 green

 orange

 pink

 purple

 blue

 black

Parts of the body

ear
eye
nose
mouth
arm
elbow
hand
leg
foot

hands

feet

Shapes

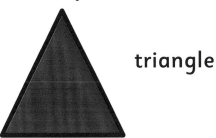 triangle

 circle

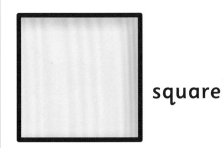 square

Prepositions

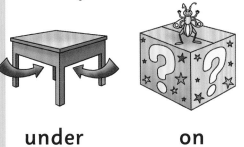

under   on   in

Direction

up   down   around

77

Animals, fish and insects

 cat

 cow

 ant

 duck

 dog

 dinosaur

 horse

 hippo

 hedgehog

 monkey

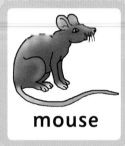 mouse

 tiger

 turtle

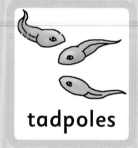 tadpoles

 snake

 seal

 insect

 octopus

 ostrich

 parrot

 pig

 penguin

 puppy

 goat

 elephant

 kangaroo

 fish

 walrus

 fox

 zebra

Food and drink

 cake

 apple

milk

 mushrooms

 sandwiches

 nuts

 orange

 ice-cream

 yoghurt

 grapes

 egg

 rice

 juice

 vegetables

water

Rooms

bedroom

sitting room

kitchen

bathroom

79

Verbs

sit

stand

point

listen

draw

paint

sing

write

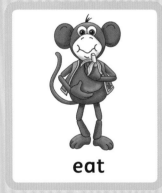
eat

drink

jump

sleep

Blending words

dad	on	duck	run
cat	ten	ducks	fun
sad	up	sun	bed
in			red

80